Riding
from the
Heart

Sheryl Lynde

Fulton Books, Inc.
Meadville, PA

Published by Fulton Books 2021

All biblical citations were taken from the Life Application Bible.

ISBN 978-1-63860-656-7 (paperback)
ISBN 978-1-63860-657-4 (digital)

Printed in the United States of America

CONTENTS

.

A NOTE TO THE READER

In this book, I share some of the strategies and approaches I have used to train the more challenging horses I have known. The methods I use are based first on building a solid foundation, incorporating effective teachings from mentors whose shoulders I stand upon today and, most importantly, from the horses themselves. This isn't necessarily a technical how-to book; however, you may learn quite a bit, and I hope you do. It is my attempt to take the mystery out of identifying and providing solutions to unwanted horse behaviors by comparing them to personal glimpses of my life. The parallels between human and horse gave me tremendous insight to the cause of many of these behaviors, as well as creating a career path I believe to be my life's purpose.

I have been a horse trainer since 2004. In that time, I have trained hundreds of equine souls and have found there is a shared space that exists among humans and horses in ways I could never have imagined. In my experience, a horse's rehabilitation depends upon his or her rider to not only take the time to listen and observe but also provide solace and empathy—all this in order to devise a personalized approach for each horse. This book explains the how and why of my training practices.

ACKNOWLEDGMENTS

Above all else, I give thanks to God. Proverbs 3: 5–6 reads, "Trust in the LORD with all your heart, lean not on your own understanding. In all your ways submit to him, and he will make your paths straight."

I dedicate this book to my daughter, Sarah. Unknowingly, she has been my navigator, lighting dark corners and steadying my balance while on unstable footing. She has always been my inspiration to want to be better and to do better.

I would like to thank my mom, who has always been our prayer warrior and remains the backbone of the family.

I have been a contributing columnist for the *California Horsetrader* magazine for the past eight years, but my relationship with them has spanned the entirety of my career. I would like to sincerely thank them for all they have done and continue to do to support all of us in the equine industry. Both Warren and Lori Wilson are the heartbeat of the community.

I would also like to thank Michelle Mason of Captured Moments Photography. She arrived as a client and left as a friend. She has documented my career through her pictures and perceptive eyes. I am so grateful for the story she has helped me tell.

And to my niece, Scarlett, listen to your heart's desires. God trusted you with the love of horses; serve them well.

CHAPTER 1

Your Life's Purpose

Gypsy Chic

D o you know your life's purpose? We have our basic needs for survival—shelter, food, clothing, transportation, etc. But according to Abraham Maslow, in addition to being able to provide basic needs for ourselves and loved ones, at the top of the list is self-actualization, the ability to realize, grow, and contribute in a way that makes a positive impact in this life. To feel valued and to realize our full potential is a critical component to our sense of self-worth. We are all unique individuals, and not being true to who we are creates an inner resistance resulting in the culmination of behavioral issues. The same applies to our horses. They are all individuals with different needs and abilities.

Like most of us, I was concerned with making a living. I kept my head down and feet moving, chasing goals that held promises of fulfillment, but ultimately, once obtained, they held no value. I was existing, not living.

I stumbled down paths that were not meant for me. I had dreams and aspirations, but I never spoke of my ambitions for fear that someone would affirm the impossibility of them coming to fruition. I was tugging on the reins; I was in flight mode. But if you have faith, God will offend your mind to reveal your heart.

After a long and successful career with owner Elizabeth Kretz in Reined Cow Horse, Gypsy Chic is now retired and getting reintroduced to a new life, a new path.

The Pasture

Some years ago, I found myself in a crisis. I was not aware of it and was thus unable to affect it, but its impact was quick, sudden, and life changing. I was living in Southern California, working as a title representative. One morning, I was sitting at a stoplight on my way to work. I glanced at the driver in the car to my left. She stared ahead, her face expressionless. One hand gripped the steering wheel, and the other clasped a cup of coffee. Her hair was perfectly styled, and her clothes professional, the armament of a fellow warrior poised to do battle for another day. But her face was strangely expressionless. Her eyes revealed a dullness, a lack of life from within, and I saw myself in her vacant and glazed expression.

The title insurance industry had been good to me for over ten years. I was divorced and a single mother. It provided my daughter and me a comfortable existence and security. Title insurance is an extremely competitive business. There were twenty-four title companies in my territory, calling on the same real estate agents, lenders, and escrow companies peddling the same product. I was usually in the top three in market share, recruited by competing companies, and earned an income that exceeded all previous earnings.

I was making a living but losing my soul. I clung to the security of a lucrative position as it afforded me more "things" that I felt I deserved and more places to run to escape the emptiness of a lifestyle that society deemed fulfilling, but it wasn't for me. My heart was never in it. If we learn to lean into uncertainty, stop worrying about whether or not we have the ability to go after a dream or desire that is in our heart, we may just find that the truest sense of security comes from being who we were created to be.

We have a choice, but the horse does not.

My crisis hit one day when I was asked to pick up loan documents from an escrow company about an hour's drive outside my territory in a rural area. As my destination approached, I slowed my pace, taking time to soak in the scenery. A pasture on my right caught my attention.

I pulled over and rolled down my windows. I felt the breeze brush against my cheeks. It was the same soft, warm gust that moved so effortlessly through the leaves of trees. A hawk caught a wind current, and he was effortlessly lifted higher in the sky as if he was being commandeered by a master puppeteer. I stepped out of my car. I left the pavement and stood on soft dirt. I looked down at my feet. Where I once felt black and white, I felt a rush of color bringing immediate awareness—all my senses came alive at once. In the midst of this scene were three horses lazily grazing while their tails moved in rhythm back and forth, keeping vigilant against flies. Everything was balanced, authentic, and genuine. There was a flow, no resistance. Nothing was trying to be something it was not. It was visceral. I was overcome with emotion; I wept. It was as if I was in the company of an old friend whom I hadn't seen for some time—an old friend who looked at me with warmth and acceptance. I hadn't realized how emotionally bankrupt I was until I felt that gaze.

> *"For I know the plans I have for you," declares the Lord, "plans to prosper you and not to harm you, plans to give you hope and a future." (Jeremiah 29:11)*

It was time I embraced who I was created to be and take a step of faith onto the path meant for me to follow. Transitions are made one step at a time.

Transitions

I ride for the joy it brings me. When I throw my leg over the back of a horse, I feel I have come home, for this is who I am. I connect with this being that has allowed me on its back. All distractions cease to draw my attention. I'm in the moment and in my purpose. There is a flow of movement, an exchange, an open conversation.

Nu Royal Remedy

Your horse has a purpose as well, and it might not be what you envisioned.

I've had horses come to me over the years that were not thriving in the discipline they were being used for. I have a gelding that I purchased as a yearling. He was bred for working cows. Even though he had the ability to be great at it, he just didn't apply himself. He didn't have the heart for the job. He held back. His movements were perfunctory and lacked the personality I knew he had. I had to continually push him, which was laborious and defeating for us both. Eventually, his eyes began to glaze and lose their character. I recognized that look. I've felt it, and it's soul crushing.

His heart was not in it. I saw it when I went into his stall. Where once his character shouted his presence, his stall was now simply a source of confinement, and he looked very small. He had the talent, but he lacked the desire for the job. Horses just like my gelding came to me from all different disciplines, from dressage to cutting. Their symptoms varied. Some bucked and reared upon entering the arena while others quit in the show pen, refusing to take direction from their trainer. But the cause was the same. They didn't have the heart for what they were being used for regardless of their breeding.

I used to run marathons, not for the love of running—I can't say that I ever did—but for the mental discipline, the challenge. I was part of a team, and we shared a formidable bond as we ran up 13,000-foot summits in Colorado and over mountain passes from Ouray to Telluride. The races were brutal, 26.2 miles of testing our mental determination, pushing through the pain of physical fatigue and fighting the urge to quit with each mile. We were at our peak of fitness. We worked hard and prepared for each marathon, but it was a pace we couldn't maintain over a length of time, not only physically but mentally. Now, if I had someone on my back, spurring me to go faster, further, again and again, I can assure you, they wouldn't be there for long.

This is where unwanted behaviors present themselves. When the human is inhabiting a life outside of who they are, something dark will eventually manifest in their personality. Anxiety or anger thrives in this environment. Depression sets in, and efforts to numb the pain are seen through symptoms such as overeating, overdrinking, and overspending. We dig deep to make it through the week, and we live for the weekends. We are constantly bombarded by society's values and its definition of success, such as the need for accumulation of possessions, position, and status. In our quest for happiness through materialistic acquisitions, we lose ourselves. We are promised happiness, but we find we have sacrificed fulfillment for complacency and contentment for envy. We become anxious and yearn for approval. But from who and at what cost?

Watching a horse that is bred to perform in a specific discipline and loves his job is seeing pure artistry in motion. It's like a symphony, each movement flowing seamlessly into the next with both horse and rider working together as a team, contributing to each other's success in the task at hand.

I am both inspired by what is possible and filled with respect for the time and effort that the rider and horse have dedicated to their craft.

But when the horse lacks heart for its job, it will develop unwanted behaviors, which will increase in severity if a change or correction is not made. The training necessary to perform at a certain level requires years of exercise and preparation, running through a repetitive sequence of patterns and maneuvers. This requires dedication and a special mindset. Its breeding is not a guarantee for success because each horse is an individual. There are a myriad of behaviors that may surface such as weaving in their stall, which is mindlessly shifting their weight from the left foreleg to the right in endless repetitions. Bucking and rearing are common as is quitting in the show pen, which is termed learned helplessness, as evidenced by the glazed eye.

So how can I best serve my gelding and still honor his inherent skills and abilities? He thrives when he is presented with a variety of challenges. He loves riding in the mountains on varying terrain. We do all that we did in the arena, just in a new arena—one without fences. We do rollbacks around brush and lead changes on level paths, and we work on transitions and stops wherever the opportunities present themselves. He needs stimulation because of his breeding and mindset, so I have to keep him engaged or he can become easily bored, leading to other negative behaviors such as unnecessary spooking episodes due to a lack of attention. We still work cattle when the opportunity presents itself, but if repetitive training is required to tighten up a specific maneuver, he will eventually shut down. I have learned to interject variety into our program. I still tune him up, but I look for improvement, not perfection. There is always tomorrow. This is not what I had envisioned for us when I purchased him, but I am well positioned to identify a horse or a human being out of their integrity. I no longer have to coerce or urge him to perform a task. Riding him on his true path aligns his purpose with his heart and mind.

I really enjoy him. He is rich in personality, and I almost lost the best part of him—his heart.

The Eyes

When you work with horses, their eyes will tell you everything. They are the windows into their souls. Just like the lifeless eyes of the woman at the stoplight, the eyes of horses will reveal fear, chaos, aggression, or detachment the moment they feel it.

With horses, the eyes reflect their true inner being. They don't mask or hide their emotions, unlike humans who are ever vigilant against vulnerability. Humans may try to disguise pain with an attempt at a smile; however, their eyes don't match the smile. With humans, there's an incongruity—you see it, you feel it.

Working with horses isn't about noticing big changes in demeanor or performance. It's about observing the subtleties, small hints of discontent, and catching that before it develops into bigger behavioral issues. I speak from experience.

CHAPTER 2

The Durango Pull

M y upbringing was not conducive to horse ownership, but if the love of horses is written on your heart, you find a way for them to become a part of your life. God knows our hearts' desires because He put them there. Moving to Durango, Colorado, was a turning point for me and the beginning of a completely different life directed by a series of synchronicities. In hindsight, I see it as God working in the background to set me on the path He had meant for me to follow. It's as if we are the tiniest of beings, smaller than an ant, and living our lives on an intricately woven tapestry of boundless proportions, oblivious to the design. Only from far above can we look down from the clouds and see the awe-inspiring beauty of its pattern. The interwoven threads representing our lives connect us to one another, and we all play an integral role in each other's lives.

Realizing the need to make a change in my life, I had reached out to my girlfriend Sandy, who was in the staffing industry at the time. She had extended her hand and offered me a way out. She took me under her wing and trained me in human resources, specifically recruiting. Neither she nor I could know how these skills would benefit me in finding my purpose. Recruiting is a riding analogy. A successful hire is a matter of making sure a candidate matches the culture of a company, just like a rider's ability and personality have to match those of the horse. After arriving in Durango, I began my job search. I was told by a local staffing company that in terms of salary and benefits, the ideal organization to work for in the area was the Southern Ute Indian Tribe. The only opening available at that time happened to be a position for recruiter. I applied and was hired. And so began one of the most incredible times of my life, filled with lifelong friendships, opportunities, and a path that would ultimately lead to my career of training horses.

A pasture epiphany, a new career, and a new life in Durango, thanks to my friend who unknowingly played a pivotal role in setting me up that way.

"Each friend represents a world in us, a world possibly not born until they arrive, and it is only by this meeting that a new world is born," said Anaïs Nin.

Whispers

Wise men and women are always learning,
always listening for fresh insights.

—Proverbs 18:15

I met incredible people in Durango. I was welcomed into the fold, and I discovered a new definition of *community*, a connection whose smile matched the eyes. The memories are rich with sustenance. They have weight and give me warmth when I visit the place they occupy in my heart.

It was in Durango that I purchased Lil' Joe, the horse that would occupy the biggest part of my heart. My mare had suffered an injury, and her recovery was lengthy. I needed another horse to ride while she recovered.

Lil' Joe has been the most significant horse in my career. He went from being my biggest challenge to my greatest asset. He was an integral part of my training program and a loyal companion. He was four at the time I purchased him; he is now twenty-five. In the beginning, I allowed some behaviors to go uncorrected. As many riders do, I kept trying to ride through the behavior, but there was no improvement. I was simply taking the issue with me whenever and wherever I rode. There were whispers that I ignored.

Sometimes, we just aren't aware; the whisperings of malcontent are soft and easily dismissed. The change can be so insidious in nature, a slow but gradual departure from your path, eventually becoming so evident that you can no longer ignore it. Pain is a great motivator.

The Human Parallel

There were two significant relationships in my life. My first marriage was brief, but from that union, my daughter was born.

The second was a long-term relationship that spanned twenty years. We were both broken for different reasons. The years were marked by a series of endless separations and fragile reconciliations. The separations were painful; the reconciliations were a cause for celebration. It was as if we had been given a lifeboat each time we reconciled; however, I knew that in reality, it was merely a raft without an anchor, at the mercy of changing currents and unpredictable swells. We did our best to hold on. We were bound together by a delicate strand of hope for what the relationship could be. Even through all of our separations, neither of us wanted to sever that bond because it was the only semblance of purity of a relationship that either of us had. But over the years, it became frayed, worn by the stress and tension we put on it. Finally, the pain of continuing outweighed the pain of leaving. That strand of hope was broken, and we were no more.

We are blessed with instinct and intuition. We pray for wisdom but remain deaf to the inner whispers and numb to the tugs and nudges telling us that something is awry. It's similar to a company and its stock. The stock is a symptom and a reflection of the internal well-being of the company itself. When stocks are on the rise, it reflects a healthy company internally. But when stocks plummet, that is a reflection of discord from within. What keeps you in the game is your level of investment. You hope the stock will rebound, but you may have invested in a shell, a fragile pretense of your hopes. The company that was once highly recommended by financial analysts is now being investigated for its fraudulent practices. The stock freefalls. When do you sell? When it hurts too much to hold on. The first initial decrease in value sets off internal alarms. The slow decline is insidious until it reaches a point where you can no longer ignore the issue. Pain is a great motivator. Listen to the whispers, no matter how faint. Each decision we make either strengthens the foundation we build our lives on or weakens it. Our instincts and intuition are products of God's grace, a compilation of lessons learned. They reveal your true path.

Several clients revealed to me after they dropped off their horses that the last time they rode, they felt something was awry. The symptoms were there—the overreactive behavior, the wrenching of the tail, and the whites of the eyes showing. There was a wreck in the making, but they chose to ride anyway. They got away with it yesterday and the day before that and the day before that, but they had been lucky. Those had been stolen rides. They quieted all the alarms and warnings. The behavior does not stay at the level at which it originally presents itself. It grows, sometimes slowly, sometimes exponentially, until a wreck ensues. It is after the rider is injured, when the pain is so great, that they seek help.

Lil' Joe was the impetus for my seeking help, which ultimately led to my life's purpose. I consider pain the ultimate motivator because I've experienced it myself, with Joe, my father, and with other areas of my life. Experience is also how we learn about others and how we develop empathy. If you've walked that same walk, you recognize it in someone else.

Auspicious Beginnings

Lil' Joe had been used as a rope horse. His previous owner told me he was finished on both ends, meaning he could head and heel. He was able to put the rider in position to rope a steer at the head as well as from behind.

But that wasn't the use I had in mind for him. I wasn't, nor had I ever been, a roper. I just wanted a good-minded, all-around ranch horse. Lil' Joe was stout and had the demeanor I was looking for. It wasn't until I started to ride in the arena that a battle ensued. When I asked for his right lead, he would stay in it for a few paces, then drop out. At first, I gave him a pass. Perhaps it was me; I wasn't asking in a way that was clear. So I asked more firmly, and he responded by kicking out. As a heel horse, he would come out of the box on his left lead. He was encouraged and trained to do so. That lead had become his lead of choice. Looking back, I see the mistakes I made. Instead of breaking it down and getting better control of his hindquarters which initiated the lead departures, I continued to force a right lead again, again, and again.

The definition of *insanity* is repeatedly doing the same thing and expecting a different outcome. Lil' Joe and I weren't communicating. Isn't this where all problems begin, with horses and humans alike? Communication is an exchange. In my case, I was the teacher. It was my job to listen, observe the movement and behavior of the horse, and then find an appropriate solution. An inability to listen creates a wedge in any relationship, creating cracks and rocking the foundation at its core. With Lil' Joe, my repeated attempts at getting him on that right lead were producing the opposite response to what I was looking for. I needed to back up and find another way to ask. For example, if I want my horse to side pass to the right, I cue with my left leg at the rib cage. If he moves off my leg, away from pressure and side passes by crossing over in the front and back, then he has been prepared well. But if he stumbles and doesn't know how to complete the task, I need to stop and evaluate which body part is stuck and work on exercises that free up either the shoulder or the hips. If he needs work on his shoulders, I'll isolate that body part and ask for his shoulders to move in either direction, asking for a slight crossover at first, then work up to a counter bend to both the right and the left. I'll then isolate the hips and move them off my legs in each direction. When each body part is moving fluidly and independently, I'll put my leg back at his rib cage and ask him to side pass. I will repeat isolating the body parts as often as necessary to complete the maneuver.

It's not about the actual side pass; it's about getting control of the individual body parts so when they come together as a whole, the maneuver is effortless. What I don't want to do is keep kicking him to the right if he can't perform the task. He'll either start popping up in front or exhibit other behaviors that negate the training process. It was obvious by Lil' Joe's reaction that he was becoming more frustrated with each request. He was reacting, not responding. His symptoms increased from kicking out to bucking until I hit the dirt. Once he had unseated me, every bucking episode would continue until I came off. I'd dust myself off, step back in the stirrup, and try again.

Finally, I was at a loss.

The Program

Getting a horse on a particular lead seems like a relatively simple issue to remedy, and normally, it is. It's common for horses to prefer a particular lead. If recognized early, this problem shouldn't evolve into the behavior that Lil' Joe exhibited. But if allowed for a length of time and, in his case, encouraged due to the discipline he was used for, it could and did become a major issue.

I researched several trainers and chose John and Josh Lyons. I enrolled in their certification program. I wasn't interested in becoming a trainer necessarily; I just wanted to learn how to resolve the issue with Lil' Joe.

Bucking became his go-to reaction; he used it well. During hunting season, I was riding him up in the mountains while ponying another horse. A hunter had dressed out a kill at the trailhead, and we had to ride by the remains left behind in order to enter the national forest. Lil' Joe began snorting as we walked by. I could feel his emotions build and his muscles tense. There was a wreck brewing. The end of my lead rope from the horse I was ponying unexpectedly touched him on the top of his rump. He was looking for an excuse to blow, and this surprise touch was all he needed. His fuse was lit. He started bucking, and he bucked hard. He increased with intensity until I came off. I watched as he turned to bolt but ran into a barbed wire fence. Instead of running through the fence, he stopped when he felt its pressure against his chest. I exhaled a sigh of relief; that could've been so ugly in so many ways. I stood there for a few minutes, lost in thought, breaking down what just happened.

This experience told me he was capable of making good decisions even at the height of his fear. He allowed me to approach and catch him. I gathered up the horse I was ponying and tied her to a tree. I got back in the saddle, worked Lil' Joe until he was calm, grabbed my other horse, and we finished the ride. I knew there was a great horse in there somewhere, and I was determined to find it.

The program was a huge commitment both timewise and financially, but like I said, pain is a great motivator. The program was six months of riding, and the tuition was steep. I was all in. I arrived on a Saturday and set up Lil' Joe's stall. The next day, I decided to ride him before the class began. I tried to get him on that right lead, and true to form, he bucked me clean off.

At the beginning of the first class on Monday morning, Josh announced, "By the way, if you hit the ground, you owe $50."

Well, that gave me pause. Hmmm…may have to get a loan.

The first three weeks of the program was eight hours a day of very specific groundwork, which exposed the holes in Lil' Joe's training and the reason behind his behavior. The groundwork identified the cause, and once that was addressed, the bucking, which was the symptom, was eliminated. Lil' Joe never bucked again. That taught me the importance of groundwork. The subsequent training was finding more efficient ways to get the desired result. When I ride, whether I'm out in the mountains or in the arena, I am always asking for a specific lead. I determine which lead my horse departs on to ensure a well-balanced horse. Lil' Joe was so uncomfortable getting on the right lead that his refusals went from mild, which in the beginning was breaking gait from a lope to a trot, to severe, which was bucking until I came off. And instead of getting control of his hindquarters, which initiated the lead, I had put the goal before the preparation. I was focused on the outcome rather than taking the steps needed to get him balanced. Don't force what isn't working; break it down and rebuild. By the end of that first session, all the groundwork was performed equally on both sides, and Lil' Joe began to develop a more balanced way of moving. We incorporated bridle work and more technical maneuvers once the foundation had been firmly established.

I learned the importance of effective groundwork and how to take that training to the saddle. Since completion of the program, I have developed my own methods and insights and incorporated these ideas into my own program. I have learned from the hundreds of horses that have come through my barn, as well as from mentors whose advice I have sought. We all stand on the shoulders of those that have gone before us, but the common thread through all the training is the importance of building a strong foundation. Life is also a process of evolving, a continuum. Just like a stagnant pool of water can become toxic, so can we.

A trainer once told me that if I come back a year later for another training session and he is still teaching the same thing, I need to find myself a different trainer. Training is always evolving, and it never stops; we are always adapting. Training takes time and dedication. By addressing and correcting the little things, you avoid having to ride the turbulent times, like the buck, the bolt, and the rear. Anything can happen when we put our foot in that stirrup, and knowledge minimizes the inherent risk we take. Don't let pain be your motivation to make a change.

Me and Lil' Joe, after completion of the program

Looking Forward

Lil' Joe and I emerged from the program as a team. Training became a new direction for me. In the beginning of my career, Lil' Joe and I performed demonstrations throughout the surrounding areas in order to build my business and attract clientele. Our demos consisted of bridleless exhibitions as well as how to execute specific groundwork to address certain behavioral issues. He moved with grace and beauty. We never left a venue without somebody complimenting him. He was well disciplined, and he exhibited his talents with the lightest of cues.

As my business grew, so did his role in my career. He gave confidence to many a fearful rider who had suffered serious injuries. As I worked with horses sent to me that had been involved in various wrecks with their owners, I resolved the issues with the horses while Lil' Joe carried the riders to heal their injuries on the inside.

If a rider habitually hung onto their horse's mouth by pulling on the reins, creating issues such as head tossing, I sat them on Lil'

Joe in the round pen and removed the bridle. Without the use of their hands, they developed an independent seat and learned to balance using their seat and legs instead of their hands.

Lil' Joe, hands free

We ponied many an insecure colt and troubled horse. When we came upon something unexpected, I could see the colts' anxiety rise and their muscles tighten. But they looked to Lil' Joe for his reaction, as he was the example they would follow. I watched as through his calm demeanor, each horse I ponied relaxed, lowered their head, softened their eyes, and took a deep breath.

Lil' Joe and Zoey owned by Kristen May

Lil' Joe and I are both on the other side of life now. We have more behind us than in front. We are both a bit grayer now, and we feel our age on cold mornings. How do you express gratitude to a companion such as this, one that has been beside you every day for over twenty years?

Lil' Joe, my greatest asset

I think it was Rick Warren that said, "Failure is not final unless you give up."

Lil' Joe didn't come to me with his behavioral issue; I created it through a lack of knowledge. He was the catalyst that prompted me to enroll in the certification program, and when I did, I was forty-eight, and forty-nine when I graduated in 2004. You are never too old to learn. During all those years of training that followed my completion of the program, I can say that Lil' Joe has remained my best horse, my favorite.

He has my heart.

Oh, what a ride it's been—one from the heart.

CHAPTER 3

Awareness

Who determines the value of a horse? Is it the price somebody has paid for him, his breeding, or his accolades?

Each horse that came to me was of equal value. Regardless of their price tag or accolades attributed to them. Each one came with an issue to be addressed.

They came from all different disciplines. From dressage to jumpers and cow horse to trail, they were all of equal value. They had been referred by previous clients, by trainers, and by veterinarians. They came for help, and help was what they all received.

Getting started

Developing trust

Years ago, I remember Sarah went to her dad's for Thanksgiving. I hadn't made alternate plans, so I made a date to bring dinner to a place called The Bridge. It was a group home for teenagers under the age of eighteen who were referred through child welfare services and probation departments.

The teenagers' offenses did not warrant being sent to Juvenile Hall; however, they were removed from their home. The Bridge provided shelter from the streets. One kid had visited his mother the day before because it was his birthday. She had dumped all his belongings on the front lawn, and when he showed, she set fire to his things. And that was just one of the stories. I spent most of the day and early evening with them. At first, they didn't acknowledge my presence. Like a herd of horses, there is a pecking order, a hierarchy. I wasn't instantly welcomed into their inner circle. They were taught boundaries, respect, and manners at The Bridge; however, they were guarded and suspected my intentions. I allowed them to approach me on their own terms. I noticed a ping-pong table, so I grabbed the paddle and started hitting the ball against the table. One by one, they came out, and they eventually warmed. Several games of ping-pong broke the ice.

By evening's end, one of the boys looked at me and asked, "Why are you here? Don't you have some place better to be for Thanksgiving?"

My heart broke because I recognized that sense of unworthiness and the pain that was behind it. But what was worse, I knew how much it took to get over it. I saw his pain; his misperception of feeling unworthy was clearly defined in his eyes. I replied, "I can't think of a better place to have been today. Thank you for sharing this day with me."

There's internal pain and external pain. The external pain can be evidenced by the wearing of a cast, a crutch, or a wheelchair. People can see that pain, empathize, and offer a hand in opening a door, picking something up that was dropped, or even financial help. But internal pain is something nobody on the outside can see. It hides in different places and reveals itself through behavioral issues, which are often misunderstood.

Preparing Love, the mustang, for her first ride

Symptoms may be defiance, uncontrolled anger, or disrespect—the list goes on. But those are symptoms, and the cause is pain.

Pain is like an invisible garment that is ill-fitting, but you've had it all your life; it gives you a sense of security because it's what you know. You accessorize it with adornments such as thoughtless, unkind comments; broken promises; or a betrayal by someone trusted. Each offense legitimizes the garment's existence, based on a false belief system.

Awareness brings light to the darkness. My garment constructed from a lifetime of misperceptions no longer fits me. It's worn and faded. The seams are unraveling, and it's garish adornments become too heavy. Dear God, please hear my prayer. I leave this at Your feet, and I surrender. Psalm 107:35 reads, "He turns a desert into pools of water, a parched land into springs of water."

Love, a nine-year-old mustang, came to get started in 2019. Here, she stands on unfamiliar ground, carrying the weight of a human. Instinctually, humans were considered predators to these mustangs. After preparing Love for the first ride, she has learned to accept me on her back.

The Fight Response

I always want to know why a horse does what he does. If he bucks, why? If he rears, why? Is he fearful? Why? As many behavioral issues are born of fear, it's become something I specialize in. When you have personal experience in an area, you have the advantage to identify it in others. Horses, just like humans, do not want to be afraid. Once I show them how to replace their fearful behavior with confidence, the trust we have established through the process is significant.

Sam

Horses have a fight-or-flight response. Some want to bolt from whatever stimuli they feel threaten their survival, while others will fight. If you surprise a horse by entering its stall without it being aware or reaching for its leg without preparing it for your presence, be prepared to duck. It can fire off a kick so quickly you won't know what hit you.

Horses with a strong fight response sometimes require another method of training. It's laying a horse down. The biggest misconception about this technique is that some people think it's about dominance on the human's part and submission on the horse's part. It's neither.

One youngster who came to me to get started was especially dangerous. He was a fighter. I understand vulnerability and insecurity well. I lived it; I recognize it. Fear hides in many places, and I know where to look. I want to prepare a horse well for his first ride. This little guy was only one and a half years old. He had twenty-plus years ahead of him to be ridden. It would be in these first few months to a year that would determine the quality of his life. His foundation needed to be strong because his future depended on it. I want to fill in the holes today. If I don't, they will surely reveal themselves tomorrow.

This colt was the toughest one I've started. His dangerous behavior permeated every step in the training process. He trusted nothing and no one. He fought being touched, especially his hind legs, and he was inconsistent. I may have realized success one day, only to dodge a kick the next. I just wasn't even sure if it was fair to him. There was so much fear and chaos in his eyes. Even after four months of groundwork, I couldn't sway the pattern of his thoughts. I even considered putting him down. After considerable preparation, one day, he would accept the saddle. The next day, he would break into a violent bucking episode with no thoughts of self-preservation. If I hadn't had a hold of his lead rope where I could at least redirect his path, he would have landed on top of the round corral. I never knew what to expect or what I could depend on. If he had injured himself, I wasn't sure he could have been safely doctored. I never saw him relax. I always observed the other horses in the barn lying down to rest either early in the morning or in the afternoons, but never him.

So the decision was made to lay him down, and it was to be done in the safety of the round pen. It is the most vulnerable position a horse can be in. It's realizing their worst fear. Horses don't think in shades of gray. Once down, he wouldn't just think he might get hurt. He would expect to die. His instincts tell him to fight and to resist. But, finally, he succumbs. Instead of death, he finds peace.

A fellow trainer safely laid him down. Once he was quiet, I lay across his rib cage, touching every area that I was unable to while he was up. I rubbed his hind legs, his ribs, his neck, and his belly for about fifteen minutes. Then I got up and left the pen. He stayed down for another thirty minutes of his own volition. When he did get up, he yawned several times and lay back down. Once up again, I went in and led him to the arena where he had more room to move about and soak in the lesson. He lay back down again for quite some time. Once he stood, I turned him out in the pasture where again he lay down of his own volition. He had defended his fears so vehemently and so fiercely for so long that once he let go of them, he was exhausted. As he lay in the pasture, the other geldings who had previously kept him at a distance now circled around him. Still, he didn't move. He no longer felt the need for his garment of vulnerability. He could finally experience peace.

Surrender—I recognized that as well.

Coming through the other side

This was the first brick laid in the foundation of trust between us. I saw who he could become.

Training takes time, and you need to take the time it takes. In this case, it took about three years, but he came through the other side. It's easy to declare a horse as hopeless and to blame it on lack of character. It releases you from trying to find a solution, especially a solution that is out of your comfort zone. But there is always someone you can rely on to get the help you need. I rode him for his first year to a year and a half of training, then turned him over to his owner who is an accomplished rider and knows him well.

His foundation has remained strong, from which his life has found a solid stronghold. His abilities can now be directed at what he was bred for, working cows, and he is magnificent to watch as he comes into his own.

Sam as he is today

Flight

The flight response is an uncontrolled reaction to fear or pain. The horse chooses flight in order to escape from a "perceived" threat to his survival.

A young horse was arriving that I was told had fear issues. I was asked to evaluate him and address areas of concern. I watched as the owner unloaded Cowboy from the trailer. She adopted a defensive posture as she walked him a short distance to my round pen, and I could see why. He was a one-thousand-pound animal ready to take flight at the slightest hint of a perceived threat in this unfamiliar setting.

Cowboy

Cowboy held his head high, pulling against the restraint of the lead rope. His eyes were wide and fixed, his breathing rapid and shallow. He lifted his feet high off the ground in a slow prance as he continually called out in hopes of hearing a reassuring response from a familiar pasture mate left behind.

Riding or leading a horse in this level of fear has the propensity to cause serious injury to both the horse and handler. His fuse was lit, and he was looking for the slightest provocation to legitimize his fear and activate his flight response.

I have seen horses whose fear overrides their instinct for self-preservation run through a fence. A flight response that is so easily triggered actually puts them at higher risk of being a danger to themselves and others. There have been instances where they have dragged or trampled their handlers who were unable to free themselves from a lead rope that had unintentionally wrapped around a leg or arm.

It isn't a matter of strength or lack of strength on the handler's part. Force is not the issue. When paired with animals of this size, the human will always lose. It's about changing their mind.

Again, I ask the question, What causes this level of fear?

Contributing factors may be pain, an injury that has gone unnoticed, or perhaps ulcers. It may be nutrition—being overfed on a diet of grain and alfalfa—or it may be a case of being underworked. His breeding may also be a factor; some performance lines are known to be more reactive than others.

Questions, possibilities, and scenarios continued to run through my mind as I observed his behavior. I allowed him to adjust to his new surroundings in the round pen for a day. He needed to acclimate. Tomorrow, training would begin.

The first day of training always starts in the round pen. It gives me insight as to what I'm dealing with. I'm able to observe their movements and look for soundness issues. It also helps me to accurately identify behaviors such as aggression, lack of respect, or simply fear. From there, I can design a program to best resolve their issues.

I knew Cowboy had been saddled and had carried a rider, but this doesn't necessarily mean that he was broke to ride. And his behavior on the ground showed me that there were holes in his training. This was not a horse I wanted to ride. When I moved him in the round pen, I noticed a disconnection. As he traveled, his attention was focused outside the pen, not on me.

He ignored my presence and cues for a change of direction and continued in his chaotic movements. Like humans, horses don't want to be afraid. I had to get his attention redirected to me in order to help him.

Have you ever been placed in a position to talk a friend off the proverbial ledge? They call because they're in crisis. They have suffered a loss of something or someone that has rocked the foundation of their world.

Sometimes, they just need a sounding board, and as you listen, you can hear the patterns of their thoughts begin to take shape and form a sensible course of action. You learn the greater their pain, the more quiet you become, the less advice you offer, and the more you listen. Eventually, they are able to work through the confusion and find new resolve. Other times though, their thoughts spiral out of control. They circle the drain, focusing on a future filled with perceived disasters.

In this situation, in order to derail their negative thought process, you want to offer a plan or solution. By breaking down the plan into smaller steps, they are able to refocus their attention to the present moment rather than a future filled with imagined calamities. They see the plan as something they can accomplish. Taking one step at a time aligns them with a different trajectory. You have their attention; you have changed their mind.

The same applies to the horse. My plan was to redirect Cowboy's focus. I changed direction in short increments by turning him toward me toward the inside of the pen. By asking in short increments, I drew his focus from the outside surroundings to me. Mindless circles may work his lungs, but I wanted to work his mind. This is where I started, and I finished when he responded to my cues.

When he faced me, I allowed him to rest, and I waited for him to exhale. The time it took for him to exhale ranged from one to ten minutes. Waiting for the exhale was key before we moved on to the next task. It was breaking up his chaotic thought process, the beginning of getting control of his emotions. If he moved off before I asked, I put him back to work, requesting more direction changes and utilizing inside turns. This was all basic groundwork that needed to be established before we moved on. This is what had been missing, the basics. I never want to excuse bad behavior due to unfamiliar surroundings. Horses may behave in the familiar setting of where they reside but come undone at a new location.

Regardless of new surroundings and all the unfamiliar distractions found therein, getting his attention was the key. There was a direct correlation between a lack of focus in the round pen and his lack of focus while being led. Whatever holes are skipped on the ground will present themselves in the saddle. The horse you lead is the horse you ride. It's all connected. Pay attention to the smaller details, and the bigger issues often resolve themselves.

When I finished a session, I wanted to see a noticeable change, and I did. Again, I don't expect perfection; I want to see improvement. I rewarded his try with a release of pressure. Sometimes, it was a thought I rewarded. Whenever I saw him using the thinking side of his brain rather than the reactive side, I released pressure. His head lowered, his eyes softened with heavy lids, and he exhaled deeply multiple times, releasing buried stress as he faced me. I wanted to be the leader he could look to for guidance and safety. It was a good start.

What was the underlying cause of Cowboy's fear? A lack of trust. I think trust is born of the heart, while fear is a result of corrupt thoughts that take over the mind.

He needed a leader, someone that said, "It's okay to be afraid, but let's complete this task, then the next." Soon, he was focused more on the tasks I was asking him to perform than on his fear.

Each day uncovered a new layer where fear was hiding. The training progressed as we uncovered and addressed each issue. He presented the lesson that he needed help with each day. I may have had a plan in mind for the day's lesson, but once training began, he would reveal his own issue, and I changed my plan to fit his needs. My only agenda was to give him the time he needed to address each issue he presented. That's it.

Each day, I made sure the corrections were given with the same calm demeanor that I had displayed the day before. Any erratic behavior on my part would cause him to be insecure and suspicious of my intentions, and the training would stall. I wanted to be the safe place he was looking for and could rely on. Consistency from me strengthened our bond, and he started making levelheaded decisions, which I richly rewarded with praise. Slowly, as he opened his heart, his fear began to turn to trust.

When I took the training to the saddle, I had to go slow as well. He easily became frustrated, and when he did, he would start to rear. So I broke down each exercise into smaller steps that he could accomplish, just as I had on the ground.

I worked on softening him laterally to counter his attempts at rearing.

While on the ground, I would drag a soft cotton rope from the saddle and allow it to touch his hindquarters as he performed outside turns. He went from kicking out and bolting to softly accepting the unexpected touch on his hind legs.

While in the saddle, I also dragged a rope and began to swing it overhead and eventually was able to rope a steer. I just kept adding layers in very small increments.

Getting softness laterally

Introduction to cows

It takes years to build a horse, and you do it one ride at a time. Cowboy progressed from a horse you couldn't trust to lead to a gentleman that walked alongside me on a loose lead rope. He learned that who held that lead rope and whom he carried on his back was his safety, so there was no need to run.

He is always better today than he was yesterday. He won my heart not because of his breeding (there isn't anything especially stellar in his lineage); not because of his monetary value (he hasn't won any ribbons or garnished any accolades); nor is he especially handsome; but because of his heart. He is all try, and I know it is born from the trust we have in each other.

Someone once asked me if I ever stop training. My reply was no.

Again, I refer to the size of these magnificent animals. We need to instill manners and discipline for our safety and theirs. Anything can happen, but you limit the risk of injury the more you prepare your horse. Also, Cowboy is a young horse; by the time he is in his mid-twenties, I'll be in my eighties. We can't depend on what tomorrow brings, and in the event I can no longer ride, I want to secure his future. I want him to reach his full potential and be a horse anyone would be proud to own—as proud as I am.

CHAPTER 4

Perception

By definition, *perception* is a way of regarding, understanding, or interpreting something—a mental impression. In other words, *perception* is defined as what we are seeing, and *reality* is defined as what is happening.

We have sixty thousand to eighty thousand thoughts per day, and 80 percent of those thoughts are inaccurate, false, and merely our personal perceptions of past experiences. Be aware of your thoughts because it's our thoughts that build the infrastructure of our belief system. If the thought is inaccurate, we've lived our lives on a foundation that is rooted in sand, yet it's how we have defined ourselves. We all have weaknesses. We build walls around them to keep them hidden. Humility isn't denying or suppressing our strengths. It's embracing our weaknesses and bringing them into the light. It is through our weaknesses that we learn empathy and are able to best serve others.

In the book *The Boy, the Mole, the Fox and the Horse*, authored by Charlie Mackesy, a boy asks, "What is the bravest thing you've ever said?"

"Help," said the horse.

My Father

My mother divorced my father when I was five. Even if it had been explained to me at the time, I doubt I would have comprehended the extent of their problem.

When my dad was in college, he had excelled in basketball. He experienced the camaraderie of a team, realizing a level of notoriety among fellow classmates not experienced by most students, and he had the adulation of fans. Perhaps the future he had envisioned for himself while in college didn't match reality after graduating. He wasn't part of a team any longer; he stood alone. There were no newspaper articles highlighting his successes and athletic prowess. Maybe he chose alcohol at that time to numb the pain of the disparity.

I can only speculate, and I wish I had the opportunity to explore it with him. But whatever the reasons, our family felt the pain of his inability to live without alcohol. The empty chair at the dinner table spoke volumes. He would come home long after we had all gone to bed. Mom would awaken and be a witness to the aftereffects of a night of overindulgence.

My mom would silently take it all in and ask incredulously, "Is this what you want for your life?"

After the divorce, we saw Dad on the weekends. I was five, and my brother Shaun was six. We would take our suitcases out to the corner and wait for his arrival.

We sat on those suitcases as the afternoon would turn to dusk, and dusk would disappear under the darkness of night. Still no Dad, but we sat and waited. Streetlights came on, and stars filled the sky. And still we waited. My perceptions were that he came, finally, and all was well. But in reality, we would eventually give up our post and yield to Mom's repeated requests to come in. He would make it the next morning, or if he did come on the scheduled evening, he was in no shape to drive. My brother Paul would take the wheel and drive us all to Dad's. There weren't any explanations. Nothing was discussed, and we went on with the weekend as if nothing happened. All was well in suburbia.

My brother Greg recalled a memory to Paul about the time he had been picked to pitch a game for his Little League team, which was huge for him. Dad had said he would be in the stands to cheer him on. The day of the game arrived, and Greg was excited to represent his team as the pitcher and proud that his dad would be there to share in this momentous event. After a couple of innings, things went awry, and Greg was pulled from his position. He was crushed, and he cried as he walked off the field. He knew Dad was watching, and he wanted so badly to perform well. Dad met Greg as he came off the field and put his arm around him to give him solace.

Paul listened quietly to Greg as he recalled his story, and when he had finished, Paul replied, "Greg, that wasn't Dad. He didn't make it to the game. That was me."

We all have a way of perceiving things that allow us to experience less pain. Greg had convinced himself that Dad had been at his game because he couldn't bear the pain of rejection. He created another story about Dad, one he could live with, and he did for years.

I loved my dad. He wasn't a villain; he was human.

I didn't really understand alcoholism, and I just didn't understand how having a drink was more important than keeping a promise to your kid. The message I internalized was that we weren't significant enough to earn his attention. I think that's the conclusion or lie that most children would come to. People affected by alcoholism and similar diseases exist by hiding the discord it brings to families.

There were times I felt shame when being told of some of Dad's escapades from distant family members. I was taken by surprise and unaware of the extent of the incidents. I couldn't explain the shame, nor could I explain why I didn't stand up for him; he was my dad. So many years of stuffing emotions had left me unable to openly communicate on any level or accurately define what I felt. It was difficult to differentiate perceptions from reality.

When I was married and my daughter was just a baby, my dad and stepmom came by. Dad told me he had joined Alcoholics Anonymous. I was thrilled for him. He asked if I would accompany him to a meeting, and of course, I agreed. At the meeting, there was a speaker. He spoke of the pain and guilt that alcoholics felt about the destruction they left in their path. He talked about their inability to form meaningful bonds because of all the broken promises that had destroyed trust with those they loved. It was difficult for alcoholics to communicate about their sickness, and they had to numb their guilt to survive. The speaker spoke for some time, and when he finished, my dad patted my knee. And we left. I realized that was his apology. He had apologized the only way he knew how, through someone else's voice. All these years, I'd held onto false beliefs that I wasn't good enough. But it was Dad who was broken. False perceptions caused unnecessary pain that I allowed to define me. My dad is gone now. He was a kind and gentle man that did his best. And I loved him.

Not too long ago, I called my brother Paul on his birthday. He spoke of causes he was championing for his church, of keeping a friend of his in my prayers, of the progression of his restaurants, and—

"Paul," I interrupted, "thank you for protecting us when Dad couldn't. Thank you for being there when Dad wasn't…"

He continued on as if he didn't hear me.

"Paul," I said again, "thank you. Your life mattered to us."

He fell silent.

The words didn't just wash over him, repelling like droplets of water as they rolled off his back. The words landed. They penetrated and mingled with distant memories and perceptions of his own that he never shared. He was quiet for a long moment, allowing himself to feel my gratitude. Communication is not our strong suit, but every once in a while, we get it right.

> *Let all bitterness and wrath and anger and clamor and slander be put away from you, along with all malice. Be kind to one another, tenderhearted, forgiving one another, as God in Christ forgave you. (Ephesians 4:31–32)*

Paloma

All the horses that come—whether they compete, they've been abandoned, or they've spent their lives as pasture ornaments—they all teach me something new.

Paloma was a horse that belonged to Christine and Katie, my earliest clients. They secured my reputation as a trainer. But more than that, Paloma, Christine, and Katie were the ones that confirmed how inaccurate perceptions could be.

I remember where I was standing when I received Christine's call over fifteen years ago. She had been referred to me by one of her friends. I heard the concern in her voice. Her daughter Katie, who was fourteen at the time, owned a young horse, a two-year-old. Katie had purchased Paloma when she was six months old, with money that she had earned on her own. That was the agreement she had made with her mom and the owner of Paloma.

Paloma had recently been trained to get started, but the trainer's evaluation was not what they wanted to hear. Out of concern for Katie, the trainer suggested that it would be best if they sold her. Paloma was fearful and reactive and lacked self-preservation.

A horse that lacks self-preservation could run through a fence or jump off a cliff when frightened in order to escape a perceived threat. It would be best if she sold Paloma for Katie's safety. Perhaps she could be a broodmare.

I understood this advice and had given it myself to a few clients over the years. A horse and rider have to be a good match. Someone in the relationship has to have more experience than the other. If the rider is green, the horse has to have more experience than the rider. If the horse is green, the rider needs to be more experienced and seasoned than the horse. Green plus green equals black and blue. Otherwise, the rider takes a tumble, and the horse gets blamed. The trainer also knew Katie's aspirations to show and didn't feel that Paloma was the horse that would help Katie realize her dreams.

Christine was obviously pained. Paloma was a member of their family. They wouldn't consider selling her, and could I help them? Paloma's behavioral issues seemed serious. But something in the way Christine and Katie were standing by this young mare caught my attention. My fees were steep for them, and they didn't have much money. So I said that if in a month, I didn't feel that I could help Paloma, I wouldn't charge them. That gave me time to assess the situation without committing full tilt.

Paloma arrived the next day. She was a beautiful paint with markings that covered her chest in the shape of a butterfly. Katie had bathed and groomed her so diligently that her white was brilliant and glowing. I instantly liked both Katie and her mom.

Katie was an old soul; there was not an ounce of fear in her toward Paloma. I watched as she handled and led Paloma to her stall. Katie had a grace about her, and she was at ease around horses. I asked them to give me enough time to evaluate Paloma, and I would call to give them my assessment. The first couple of days, we spent in the round pen. I needed answers to my questions. The symptom of a horse's behavior might be the buck, the spook, or the rear. But what is the cause? If I work on the cause, I don't have to ride the symptoms. I saw that Paloma's fearfulness was more a result of trying hard to please. She would respond to my cues too quickly and too explosively, beyond the energy level from which I had asked. I kept the pressure and my voice low, not with the intention to tiptoe around her but to be the calm I wanted to instill in her. I had to be the example I wanted her to follow. If my energy level was a four and she responded at a level nine, I didn't increase my energy level to match hers. I stayed at the level that I was looking for her to respond within. She was overly reactive, an overachiever.

As she circled the round pen, her movements were chaotic and abrupt. She lacked focus. Her attention was equally divided between me and whatever was happening outside the round pen. I asked for several inside turns toward me in short increments, just to get her attention redirected. When she looked at me, I stopped moving. She immediately licked her lips in an overly reactive rhythm, her blue eyes staring at me without blinking and her head held high.

I remained still, waiting for her to relax. I wasn't rewarding her completion of the turn. I wanted to reward her when she became calm. To be effective in your groundwork, you must know the purpose of what you want to accomplish. She was on the muscle—nervous and tight. This wasn't the horse I wanted to ride. I stood with my shoulders relaxed and slightly turned away, and I waited. Soon, she lowered her head and blinked her eyes—fast at first—but then the blinks slowed and lingered. Finally she exhaled; that was what I was waiting for, the exhale. I stood there longer, and she exhaled more. She lowered her head a little more and relaxed her jaw.

That's when I praised her, in the stillness. There is magic in silence, that moment when you give a horse the opportunity to just be. Years ago, I heard this analogy, and it has always proven true. A musical note is just one long note. It could even be irritating if it continues in its long, monotonous sound. But when you add breaks of silence within the note, you create music.

I stood there looking at Paloma, telling her that no matter what happened in that round pen between her and me, she had the love of a young girl and her mother. Christine and Katie had her back. They were committed. They would always show up for her. How lucky she was to have that. Rest in that, trust in that.

"Just let me help you with your fear," I told her.

I am not a proponent of positive thinking. I am an advocate of awareness. Be a watcher of your thoughts. Thoughts have energy. They are the building materials used in constructing your beliefs. They change your demeanor and are expressed in how you carry yourself, how you walk, and the tone of your voice. Hold onto your beliefs with loose reins, be open to adopting a better way, and have a teachable spirit. If you find yourself defensive, ask why. Are you defending a false belief? Truth simply is and has no need of a defender.

A horse sees how you respond to it. You must be the example you want the horse to follow, and that takes awareness. I continued working Paloma, asking for inside turns and allowing her time to soak on the release, and the releases were long. I moved her feet in the direction I wanted at the speed I requested, and she obliged me willingly and calmly. There is a hierarchy in the herd. Lead horses direct and move the horses below them in a pecking order. They direct their feet. They take the space they are standing on. I became the dominant horse, not aggressively but decisively. I brought Paloma's emotions up and brought them back down in a slow, methodical pace until she trusted me to be the leader she wanted to follow and she became the horse I wanted to ride. I put my foot in the stirrup and threw my leg over and sat until she relaxed. She was still tight and fearful, but because of the groundwork, I had credibility on her back. Paloma listened and performed in spite of her fear. When I clucked to move her into a trot, she jumped at the sound but didn't carry her fear any further. Instead of bolting, she moved off into the gait I requested. That was an excellent decision. Christine and Katie's faith were well placed in her. I smiled to myself as I rubbed her neck. I told her she was going to be fine.

I called Christine and told her only that she and Katie should come up. We set a time, and they arrived the next day to watch my session with Paloma. Both were quiet, solemn, and unsure of my findings. They were bracing themselves, apprehensive of what I had to say regarding Paloma's future. I showed them all the groundwork, the transitions, the stops, and the attention she gave me. They recognized the change in her demeanor; she was calmer. Then I rode her at all her gaits, stopped, stepped off, looked at Katie, and asked if she would like to ride her horse. I stayed in the pen. I watched Paloma's eye as Katie climbed up. There was no change; her softness remained. Katie had been her handler since she was six months old. She had halter broke Paloma and even showed her in halter classes. I didn't need to chaperone. Christine began to cry as Katie grew a smile that matched the joy in her eyes. She rode her horse for the first time. She took Paloma through her paces, and Paloma willingly performed. It was Paloma's turn to carry Katie. They were a team.

I'm not sure how Paloma's fear had originally manifested. She had suffered an injury in her stall early on. When Katie arrived at the barn after school, all she found were the remnants of a leg strap to her blanket that was caught in the wire mesh fencing of the stall. She had been entangled and panicked. She put her leg through the fence, causing multiple lacerations that required innumerable stitches and stall rest. After rehabilitation, she became more reactive until her fear level was a concern for those around her. Fear doesn't usually stay compartmentalized. If left unattended, it grows and attaches itself to any stimulus. Even what once had been accepted prior to the accident was no longer trusted.

It can happen with humans as well, particularly after healing from an accident that took you by surprise and caused serious injury. You feel a bit more vulnerable and can become more reactive at perceived threats, unnecessarily jumpy, and easily frightened.

Paloma stayed with me for a little over ninety days, and so did Katie. She did chores, cleaned the barn aisles and stalls, assisted me with clinics, and loped some of the horses I had in training, all so she could be close to Paloma. She wanted to learn everything she could. She learned what to ask of Paloma, how much pressure she could use, how to build her confidence, and how to respond versus react. We worked through my program on the ground, speed control, transitions, and stops. We took what we taught Paloma from the ground to the saddle and improved on them: smoother transitions, shoulder control by counter bending, reverse arch circles, diagonals, and side passing. We worked on turning on the forehand, turning on the haunches, lead departures, and working over poles.

I taught Katie how to ask the right questions and how best to help Paloma thrive. I taught her not to start with a goal but to break it down. Another day was spent getting control of the hips, which enables the rider to get correct lead departures. Katie learned how every step we take is to lay the foundation for the next maneuver.

"Don't look down, Katie. That's where you will land. Don't look at her head." When I drive my truck, I told her, "I don't stare at the hood. Look in the direction you're heading. Just like thoughts construct your beliefs, beliefs direct your path. Look where you want to go, and Paloma will follow. Be as firm as necessary, but as light as possible."

Katie listened. She watched, and she had an unyielding capacity to learn. As a result, Paloma progressed. She was sensitive and responded well to a minimum amount of pressure from the seat and legs. Once she got it, you had to move on. There was no need to drill. She needed variety to stay engaged. I loved riding her. She was smooth, and she felt like she was floating above the ground as she moved out. Because of Katie's devotion to her, I spent whatever extra time I had with Paloma. We hauled her up to the mountains where we used trees for our serpentine patterns, clearings for loping circles, and felled trees for jumping. Paloma adjusted to every environment beautifully.

We took her to an equestrian center during an event. I cruised around, getting her exposed to loudspeakers, the noise of onlookers in the stands, and horses running by her at all levels of control or lack thereof as she carried me on her back. When it came time for Katie and Paloma to go home, I knew they would be a formidable team.

They later won reserve champion in a rated APHA Hunter Under Saddle class in Temecula and went on to be successful at numerous county events for English Hunter Under Saddle and Over Fences.

Paloma, Christine, and Katie blessed my career in many ways. You can't outgive God. The change in Paloma was undeniable. Because of her, my clientele grew considerably. Paloma exhibited only her best. She exuded a new confidence. It was as if she was saying, *Look at me now.*

Paloma left her fear behind because she had people who believed in her. Paloma left the misperceptions of her value behind; she thrived in an environment where everyone who came in contact with her believed in her tremendous worth. We conveyed it in our approach, our touch, our countenance, and the tone of our voice.

My friendship with Katie and Christine and the memories of a summer spent with a little girl and her horse will remain with me always.

Katie and Paloma

CHAPTER 5

Connection

Jade, I am not a threat. This simple touch was thirty minutes in the making.

I realize now that my life change was based on a need to shift from mainstream societal values to my own. By that, I mean to something with sustenance and something of intrinsic value. I needed to find a way to serve. I wanted my life to matter. I wanted to leave something for my daughter, something that can't be seen or held—just a thought, a glimpse of the best of me that touches and mingles with the best of her. Because of my daughter, I've always wanted to do better and be better. I've certainly fumbled along the way, but I just wanted to get what matters right. I want to know that for her, in some small glimpse of my life, I mattered because no life mattered more to me than hers.

Coming from a place of intrinsic value shifts your focus from self to something else (or someone else) for a greater cause, and in doing so, you are blessed beyond measure. Extrinsic value comes from a place of getting and doing something for the reward, attention, or status. When I step up on a horse, all distractions fade, and there is a sense of awareness that fills me with exhilaration. I connect with this being. I never take for granted that I am a guest on its back, and I relish the opportunity.

Jade, introduction to a whole new world

Johann Hari is the author of *Lost Connections*. According to Hari, research has been compiled on highly materialistic people over lengthy periods. Not only has their pursuit of possessions and status not produced one inch of happiness in their lives, but they are significantly more depressed, anxiety-ridden, angry, and sickly than those that adopt a value system that seeks to serve, not get. I had everything I needed as a title rep.

As a title representative, twenty-four title companies vied for position in market share to hold the coveted number one spot. To occupy that spot brought recognition, status, and clout with your company and clients. The stress of maintaining that position wears on you. It has been proven that we as humans can tolerate a great deal if we find value in the purpose. But if the purpose only glorifies the individual, such as accumulation of material gains and status, then for me, motivation wanes, and emptiness sets in. I needed to feel as though I was making a difference, a contribution to someone else's well-being. When I ride, I'm making a connection with a thousand-pound animal that has the sensitivity to respond to a look and a thought. That's connection, and connections are imperative to our well-being whether they be through human or animal interactions.

Jade, a four-year-old, getting started. Never being off her property, she is enjoying the new scenery.

Intrinsic Value, Meaningful Connections

I was going to pick up a nine-year-old gelding that hadn't been started or, for that matter, handled on a consistent basis. He was coming for training. He had grown to over fifteen hands in height, and he knew no boundaries. When grooming, the owners would brush him from the outside of his paddock, keeping the fence in between them for security. His presence was quite formidable.

We herded him into a twenty-four-by-twenty-four pen, and it still took me almost an hour to halter him. He shied from being approached or touched, let alone being caught. But eventually, I was able to load him up in the trailer and head for home. He progressed through my program nicely. He wasn't especially fearful; he had just been calling the shots for nine years. He was in need of discipline and a job. He needed some mental stimulation. Prior to coming to me, he hadn't been off his property. I was the link to his previous life, and I became his security. I presented boundaries, which he followed willingly. He had a good mind; he was kind and sensitive. I was able to safely get him started, and he carried me easily through all the paces of training. When it was time for this gentle giant to go home, he did something that many horses did as they left my facility. As the owner was loading him in the trailer, he stopped and turned his head to look at me.

I was not easy for him to find as I was off a little to the right. But he saw me, and our eyes locked. He held my gaze for more than just a few moments.

"He doesn't want to leave," the owner commented.

It was more than that.

It was as though he was showing a heart full of gratitude. He felt safe and had a new sense of purpose with clearly defined boundaries, just as children need. I looked at him in awe, remembering that first day of trying to catch him and how far he had come in just a few months. It's that heart-to-heart connection that touches and fulfills me. By helping him, he helped me. You can't place a price on that. That's intrinsic value.

God uses our weaknesses to benefit others.

Bella was a seven-year-old thorough-bred mare that had been abandoned and had found her way to the Horse Nation Foundation program in Huntington Beach, California, headed by Dr. Carole Harris.

Carole is a psychologist that blends her rescue for these troubled horses as part of her rehabilitation program with at-risk youth. Her office has no walls. It is open; the ceiling is blue sky. This is where she brings kids from the inner city who see an expanse of space and a glimpse of the ocean

Bella

for the first time in their lives. They find themselves in a pasture setting, interacting with horses of all different breeds and all different stories, not unlike their own.

At the rescue, Bella normally stayed off in the distance, staying out of the fray, aloof. She remained unapproachable to the group. Even in her current state of being, as she remained on the periphery, she was being used to benefit others. The kids in the program observed her. They recognized her behavior. They saw themselves in her. They felt empathy, understanding, and camaraderie all at once. She became the horse the kids tried to reach the hardest but couldn't.

When Carole contacted me to get Bella started, she told me the goal was to get her suitable for adoption. Bella had earned a reputation at the barn for being difficult and unpredictable, and she lived up to everyone's perceptions of her. The more people held onto their bias, the more they postured themselves in a defensive and hypervigilant demeanor and further supported the behavior they came to expect from her. Bella obliged their expectations and confirmed their beliefs—she was untrainable.

It isn't what happened during training that was so memorable about our time together. It was when it was time for her to return to Carole.

Bella had progressed through training well. She stayed with me for about seven months. The older a horse is, the longer the training takes. They've developed their own traits and habits that have had time to mold and shape their personality. That old adage, "You can't teach an old dog new tricks," isn't exactly accurate. You can; it just takes longer. I was told once that a two-year-old usually takes ninety days to start, and that is just for the basics. For every year after the age of two, add an additional two months to your training time. With each older horse I have started, this has proven true. Be prepared to take the time it takes, young or old and troubled or not, and take one step at a time.

During the time Bella was with me, I promoted her through newsletters, articles, and social media because I believed in Carole's program. By integrating horses into her therapy program with kids, she was making an incredible impact; she was reaching them. We were able to raise awareness and funds for Bella and Carole's rescue. Clients generously donated, and my vet donated his fees for his services as well. I had suspected she had ulcers, which had stalled the progression of her training. When cinched, she began to pin her ears, clinch her jaw, and grind her teeth. She began to rear when I put my foot in the stirrup. My vet scoped her and indeed confirmed the presence of ulcers. We were able to successfully treat her, and there was a noticeable change in her behavior. Training progressed nicely, and we moved through my program without any issue after her treatment. It is always important to identify and rule out pain as a possible cause for behavioral issues. The day before Bella was to go home, I had a conversation with her as I unsaddled and led her to her pasture. I told Bella how people were supporting her, how they believed in her worth, and how incredibly far she had come. Now it was time for her to give back. She was going home, and there were some kids that would benefit from her story.

Early the next morning, I walked down to her pasture with a halter in hand. She was eating alongside a couple of my mares. Normally, she would watch me as I came toward her. As soon as I got close, she would try to dodge me for a few minutes, hiding between her pasture mates until she realized the futility of it all and would give it up. But as I opened the gate, she looked up.

I said, "Time to go, girl." I began to take a step into the pasture but stopped. She didn't play the dodge game.

She lifted her head, left her breakfast and pasture mates behind without a thought, met me at the gate, and stood quietly as I haltered her. She walked beside me on a loose lead, and I loaded her in the trailer without hesitation.

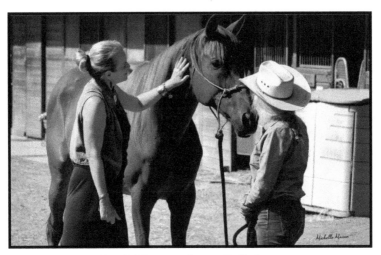

Carole Harris welcomes Bella home.

Upon arrival at the Huntington Beach Equestrian Center, she unloaded calmly and waited patiently with me as we were directed to an area where we were to perform a demonstration for the kids in Carole's program. I reflected back seven months to the day I had picked up Bella. Her head had been high, and she towered above me as I entered her stall. She was alert, nervous, and reactive, pulling against the lead rope, easily distracted by all that was going on around her. A staff member went ahead of me to diffuse any activity that may have set her off. They had been indoctrinated into the fold and believed the perceptions that had been created about her. True to form and her reputation, she bolted, pulling the lead rope from my hands and calling out to all that would listen and announcing her freedom as she ran through the endless rows of barn stalls. I tracked her down, gathered her up, and again attempted loading her in my trailer. It took some time, but we were successful. That was our introduction.

That was just seven months ago, and here she stood beside me with such grace, self-assured and composed on a loose lead, waiting for her opportunity to give back, and she did. I felt an immense sense of awe as I stood with her. I placed my hand on her neck, hoping, in some way through it, she could feel my heart and the depth of gratitude that overwhelmed me for all that she had shown me over the past seven months.

She taught me the resilience of spirit and forgiveness.

Although she was abandoned and undernourished, she rose above and became the inspiration we can all draw from.

I overheard a couple of comments from the staff at the equestrian center. They couldn't believe this was Bella. She allowed the kids to approach and touch her without fear, and she performed the demonstration beautifully as she carried me on her back.

She was the Bella I knew she could be; her life mattered.

Bella gives back.

CHAPTER 6

Leaders Are Learners

For sixteen years, I worked with hundreds of troubled horses and started young and older horses alike. I never stopped learning. With each horse, I looked forward to a new opportunity to grow as a trainer.

I've worked with tough horses and difficult clients as well as special, memorable horses and kind, generous clients. Just as with working with horses, timing is everything. I started my career late in life because for many years, I fought the path that was intended for me, but

Jimmy

once I took that step of faith, I found my purpose and a career that I truly loved. But now I find myself at an age that I need to retire from starting colts and working problem horses.

Jimmy

NOT BECAUSE I didn't think I was good enough because I've asked myself that question every day since I began working with horses. I don't think I ever thought I was good enough, but I've always given my best.

NOT BECAUSE the "business" of horse training wore me down. It did at times, but I loved what I did too much to quit. I've worked with some tough horses, and they have been my greatest teachers. I've worked with some tough owners, and because of them, I learned the only approval worthy of seeking is God's.

NOT BECAUSE I wasn't busy enough. There were times when business was lean, but just like the economy, it is cyclical. Running your own business is not for the faint of heart. During those lean years, I found strength by surrendering and letting go of trying to control my life for my purpose. I found peace serving someone greater than myself. My faith endures. My goal with training was to ensure each horse had a future by teaching them to be a respectful, safe companion that anyone would love to own. I was busier than I wanted to be.

BUT BECAUSE it's time. I'm not so much interested in building a career as I am taking the time to build a horse. This is where my heart has been all along. I am incredibly grateful to everyone who entrusted me with their horses. I hope I have served you well.

*****

I want to conclude this book with some reflections. I have been blessed by all the horses that I have trained, and each one has been a gift. The lessons I have learned, I believe, are of value to both horse people and non-horse people alike. We are not so different spiritually and emotionally. These closing remarks are not in a particular order, but they all carry significant worth.

The First Reflection Is My Mission Statement

I continue to provide guidance and boundaries because I care deeply about ensuring that each horse has a bright future. We have a duty to do right by the horse we have taken ownership of. With ownership comes great responsibility.

Instilling ground manners

Legendary equestrian Tom Roberts said, and I quote, "If you are fond of a horse and wish to do him a real favor, train him well. Teach him good manners and good habits, both on the ground and under the saddle. You never need to worry about the future of such a horse for any reason you may need to part with him."

Like the troubled youths I met at The Bridge, a horse left to his own devices has not been given the tools he needs to be the best he can be and is destined for an uncertain life. So do the right thing, honor your commitment, and provide the training your horse deserves. Your safety and your horse's future depend on it.

Teach him good manners and good habits.

How to Build Confidence and Keep It

Competence is a skill you develop over time through practice, training, and dedication.

The more thorough your preparation, the more competent you become at developing your skills.

Confidence is an emotion. It is similar to competence only in the respect that it takes practice, awareness, and diligence to be a watcher of your thoughts. Thoughts have energy; they have weight and power. They have the ability to inspire or halt your ambitions.

We all experience hardships and challenges in life that create stress. It's how we choose to move through a crisis that either develops character or weakens our resolve. We weren't created in a spirit of fear; it comes to us through invitation. We invite it into our consciousness. It can become all-consuming, permeating our behaviors, just as with horses.

Stress is an emotion, and it triggers hormones that we feel as a rush of energy through our body. When we react to someone or something, we actually become altered because there is a change in our chemical state. According to Dr. Joe Dispenza, an international lecturer, "Stress hormones give the body a rush of energy, and this rush is something we become addicted to. We relive that feeling every time we revisit the memory of that experience, and we do it over and over again. The feeling becomes familiar, comfortable. Without even being aware, our mind will drift away and we become immersed in the feelings of past mistakes and offenses. We become addicted to our thoughts."

But as we discussed, thoughts or perceptions can and do betray us. "Most people try to create a new personal reality as the same personality." It won't work. The same applies to your approach with your horse. If your horse is not producing the results you desire, you must change how you ask or cue your horse. Be open to the concept that there may be a better way to accomplish the desired result you are looking for.

In order to teach the horse a new maneuver or correct an unwanted behavior, you need to adopt different techniques from the methods that created the unwanted behaviors in the first place. Different methods create new and different results. Experiencing different results builds confidence.

Confidence is an inside job. Be open to changing how you ride. It takes work and awareness, and just like attempting to make any change for the better, it takes time and practice—a willingness to be out of your comfort zone.

On those days when you are circling the drain and you feel your progress has stalled, just stop. Meditate on what went right and live in that space, feel it and expand it. Keep your eyes on your purpose, and in the silence, the answer will come. Are you doing your best? If yes, feel that. If not, change it. Remember, leaders are learners. No worthwhile change occurs without effort and hours in the saddle.

Know When to Take the Reins and When to Release

Training a horse is a process of applying pressure and release. Too much pressure and the horse can become overly reactive, fearful, or dull. Some become desensitized to the amount of constant pressure, and usually as a result, people defer to a bit they feel is more severe. But remember, it's not the bit that is severe; it's the hands that are holding onto the reins.

Bits are tools, all designed for specific reasons. You must learn their correct uses and develop the feel to benefit from them. You teach the release. There has to be a release for the horse to get lighter. Not enough pressure or releasing too soon before getting the desired response renders the cue ineffective; you are nagging at this point. This frustrates the horse, and the horse begins to toss its head to find its own release. But just the right amount of pressure will produce the effect you want—getting the horse's attention. This takes feel. When applying pressure, you are asking the horse to give to the bit or yield a body part to the pressure of the rider's seat or leg. When you feel a try, then you release. The learning happens not from the pressure but from the release. If you are overly critical, you create a symptom called learned helplessness. Just as in people, if their effort goes unrecognized continually, they either quit trying or they become bitter and fight. Can you imagine teaching someone to be helpless? It's not about winning. It's about empowering and improving.

Trust Yourself

Humility is a by-product of failure. It's not an emotion that you decide to embrace. It comes from life experiences and from the misses in life, the times that bring you to your knees. You will never find the truth in comparing yourself to others; they have their own purpose and life to live that is separate from yours. Be you. Both you and your horse are individuals with different capacities for learning. Just be aware, listen, and observe. Always be open to learning. If you need help, seek a professional that has been recommended to you by someone whose opinion you respect. Visit the trainer and observe their methods and how the horse responds to their style of training. They may or may not align with your philosophy. And most of all, take the time it takes. Don't rush through your program; you may miss something your horse is telling you. It's not a race. Every day is a step toward your desired result, so make the most out of each step. May God shine his face on you and may you have many blessings on your path.

ABOUT THE AUTHOR

I have started colts and worked with problem horses for the past eighteen years. I have been a contributing columnist for the *California Horsetrader* magazine for the past eight years. Hundreds of horses came through my program, and with each horse, I learned. They came from all different disciplines, from dressage to cutting. I specialized in building a strong foundation, from the ground up. I discovered their strengths and enhanced those skills. Where was their heart? It wasn't always in the discipline they were bred to do. I recognized those behaviors associated with fear and aggression were merely symptoms. By discovering the cause, the symptoms resolved themselves. The toughest colts were my greatest teachers. This book highlights those and how we came out the other side—both better for the experience. I hope you enjoy it.

CPSIA information can be obtained
at www.ICGtesting.com
Printed in the USA
LVHW071509070322
712799LV00010B/176